W9-AAZ-273

Aly Raisman

Aly Raisman

ATHLETE AND ACTIVIST

ANNA LEIGH

LERNER PUBLICATIONS ◆ MINNEAPOLIS

For Alexa

Lerner Publications Company
A division of Lerner Publishing Group, Inc.
241 First Avenue North
Minneapolis, MN USA 55401

For reading levels and more information, look up this title at www.lernerbooks.com.

Image credits: Dimitrios Kambouris/Glamour/Getty Images, p. 2; Michael Loccisano/Getty Images, p. 6; Harry How/Getty Images, p. 8; Alex Livesey/Getty Images, p. 9; AP Photo/Stephan Savoia, p. 10; David Madison/Getty Images, p. 11; Tom Pennington/Getty Images, p. 13; AP Photo/David J. Phillip, p. 15; Bryan Pollard/Shutterstock.com, p. 16; Ray Tamarra/Getty Images, p. 17; Alex Grimm/Getty Images, p. 19; Tim Clayton/Corbis/Getty Images, pp. 20, 35; Julian Finney/Getty Images, p. 21; Aram Boghosian/The Boston Globe/Getty Images, p. 22; Ronald Martinez/Getty Images, p. 24; Cameron Spencer/Getty Images, p. 26; Pete Souza/The White House/Getty Images, p. 27; Paul Archuleta/FilmMagic/Getty Images, p. 28; Lintao Zhang/Getty Images, p. 30; Charles Eshelman/Getty Images, p. 31; Suzanne Kreiter/The Boston Globe/Getty Images, p. 33; Pascal Le Segretain/Getty Images, p. 34; Laurence Griffiths/Getty Images, p. 36; Craig Barritt/Getty Images, p. 37; AP Photo/DaleGYoung/DetroitNews, p. 38; AP Photo/Phil McCarten/Invision, p. 39.

Cover Image: Dimitrios Kambouris/Getty Images.

Main body text set in Rotis Serif Std 55 Regular 13.5/17. Typeface provided by Adobe Systems.

Library of Congress Cataloging-in-Publication Data

The Cataloging-in-Publication Data for *Aly Raisman: Athlete and Activist*
   is on file at the Library of Congress.
ISBN 978-1-5415-4261-7 (lib. bdg.)
ISBN 978-1-5415-4350-8 (eb pdf)

Manufactured in the United States of America
1-45419-39657-9/7/2018

CONTENTS

Aly Raisman has appeared at numerous events since making a splash at the 2016 Olympics. Here she appears at a 2018 concert at the Minneapolis Armory in Minneapolis, Minnesota.

Aly Raisman took a deep breath and stepped onto the competition floor. She smiled as she took her opening pose, but her eyes were filled with determination. It was the last event of the all-around final at the 2016 Olympics in Rio de Janeiro, Brazil. Raisman had already completed her routines on the vault, uneven bars, and balance beam. She was in third place behind her teammate Simone Biles and Russian gymnast Aliya Mustafina. Raisman was twenty-two years old, and this was her second Olympic Games—an accomplishment that few American gymnasts before her had achieved.

It was also Raisman's second time competing in the Olympic all-around final. Four years earlier, she had come up just short of the medals, finishing in fourth place after losing a tiebreaker to Mustafina. It had been a disappointing finish, and it had pushed Raisman to train even harder to make her second Olympics. She was determined to show that she was stronger than ever, and she hoped that this time, she would finish the event with a medal around her neck.

The folk music for Raisman's routine began, and she started to dance. Then she placed her heels in the corner of the floor to prepare for her difficult opening tumbling pass, a sequence of flips and twists that some had once considered impossible. Raisman took a step and launched into the pass. She flipped through the air and landed solidly in the opposite corner of the mat. The crowd roared.

Raisman continued dancing, spinning, twisting, and flipping while the crowd cheered and clapped to the rhythm of her music. She completed one powerful move after another. Then it was time for the final tumbling pass. Once again, she lined up her feet in the corner of the mat and took off across the floor. She landed one final flip, and the music came to an end. As she held her final pose, the crowd erupted into screams, and she broke into tears. She knew the routine had been one of her best. And she knew she had achieved what she had been working so hard for.

Raisman proudly displays her silver medal.

Raisman cried as she waved to the crowd. Then she ran off the floor to hug her coach, Mihai Brestyan, and wait for the judges to post her score. Biles performed her floor routine next, and Raisman cheered her on. Biles, who is known as the greatest gymnast of all time, came away with the gold medal, and Raisman took silver. But it felt like gold.

Later that night, Raisman posted a photo of herself on Twitter. In the photo, she is wearing her silver medal around her neck, and she has a big smile on her face. But the caption, written in all capital letters, said it all: "Redemption, baby."

Golden Goals

Alexandra Rose Raisman was born on May 25, 1994, in Needham, Massachusetts. She was the oldest child in her family. Her brother, Brett, was born in 1996, and a few years later, Aly's parents, Rick and Lynn, adopted

Aly's hometown displays a sign to cheer her on.

two little girls, Chloe and Madison. The family loved sports. Aly's father had played hockey and baseball, and her mom had competed in gymnastics when she was in high school. Aly was very energetic, so her mom thought it would be fun to sign up for a Mommy and Me gymnastics class at the nearby gymnastics club, Exxcel Gymnastics and Climbing. Aly had so much fun in the gym that when the class ended, her mom signed her up for another class.

Aly also took ice-skating lessons and played softball, basketball, and soccer. But gymnastics was her favorite. She loved bouncing around on the trampolines, swinging on the bars, and running around in the gym, trying out new flips and skills.

When Aly wasn't in the gym, she loved watching gymnastics competitions on TV. She would record competitions and watch them over and over again. Her favorite was a video of the 1996 Olympics, which were held in Atlanta, Georgia. That year the US women's team won the gold medal in the team competition. Aly wanted to be just like them. At eight years old, Aly decided that one day, she too would go to the Olympics and win a gold medal.

The Magnificent Seven

In 1996 the US women's gymnastics team was made up of seven women who became known as the Magnificent Seven: Shannon Miller, Dominique Moceanu, Dominique Dawes, Kerri Strug, Amy Chow, Amanda Borden, and Jaycie Phelps. Dawes, Strug, and Miller all competed in both the 1992 Games and the 1996 Games.

Kerri Strug's coach, Bela Karolyi, carries her in front of a cheering crowd after she hurt herself performing a vault in 1996.

Miller won a total of seven medals. She is still the American gymnast with the most Olympic medals.

In the team competition, the Magnificent Seven were in the lead, but then Moceanu fell on both of her vaults. The team was in danger of falling into second place. Strug was the last to compete. On her first vault, she fell and hurt her ankle. But she completed her second vault anyway. When she landed, she immediately hopped onto one foot to avoid putting pressure on her injured leg. It was a dramatic finish. The team became the first US women's gymnastics team to win an Olympic gold medal.

Striving for Success

When Aly was ten years old, she found out that two of her coaches at Exxcel would be moving to a different gym. Some of Aly's teammates talked about training at another nearby gym, called Brestyan's American Gymnastics Club. This gym was known for being tough, but it also had a very good team. Aly thought the coaches at this gym could help her reach her goal of one day going to the Olympics. She decided to begin training at Brestyan's too.

Right away, Aly told her new coach, Mihai Brestyan, that she wanted to go to the Olympics. He took her seriously. He could see that she was a hard worker and that she loved gymnastics. With these qualities, he knew she would go far. Brestyan told Aly that she would have to work very hard and become very serious about gymnastics. This meant training hard, getting enough rest, and eating healthful foods. She also couldn't take time off for vacations. Aly was up for the challenge.

Aly began working hard every day in the gym. In the summer, when her friends and family went on vacation, she spent even more time in the gym perfecting her skills. She was working toward becoming an elite gymnast. At this level, she would be able to compete in international competitions.

In 2009, when she was fourteen years old, Aly became an elite gymnast. Then she competed at her first US Junior National Championships. She finished in third place and officially earned her spot on the junior national

Mihai Brestyan, Aly's longtime coach

team. This meant she would attend monthly national team training camps at Karolyi Ranch in Texas, and she would be able to participate in competitions such as the World Championships and the Olympic Games.

A few months later, Aly was selected to compete in her first meet: the Junior Pan American Championships in Aracaju, Brazil. Aly won four medals at this competition. Aly's team won the gold medal, Aly came in third in the all-around, and she won gold medals for her routines on vault and floor.

Karolyi Ranch

In 1981 gymnastics coaches Bela and Martha Karolyi moved from Romania to the United States. The couple bought land near Huntsville, Texas, and began building up a ranch. They turned an old barn into a gym and began hosting training camps for gymnasts in 1984. They later built two more gyms and dorms where gymnasts could stay. The ranch is also home to animals such as camels, peacocks, horses, and deer.

The Karolyis coached the Magnificent Seven in 1996, and by 2000, the ranch had become the official training center of the US national team. In 2011 it became the Olympic training center. Martha Karolyi was the national team coordinator from 2001 to 2016. She observed gymnasts at monthly training camps and competitions. It was her job to choose which gymnasts would compete in major competitions, including the Olympics.

The Karolyis' program produced many great gymnasts. However, training at the Karolyi Ranch was intense, and Martha was intimidating. Many gymnasts were afraid to make any mistakes. They didn't want to lose their chance of going to the Olympics. Some gymnasts complained that the food and medical care at the ranch were not good enough to meet the needs of top athletes. In 2018 USA Gymnastics stopped holding training camps at the ranch, and the ranch closed down.

A sign points to Karolyi Ranch, the legendary facility where Aly trained.

Aly's success continued in 2010, when she was selected to participate in major competitions in the United States, Italy, and Australia. She also competed in the World Championships in the Netherlands, where the US team won a silver medal.

The next year, Aly competed at the World Championships again. This time, they were held in Tokyo, Japan. She competed with teammates Jordyn Wieber, McKayla Maroney, and Gabby Douglas. It was Aly's second time at the World Championships, but her teammates were there for the first time. They began coming to Aly for advice. She knew it was her job to encourage the team. Under Aly's leadership, the US team won the team gold medal. Aly and her teammates had become World Champions.

Olympic Hopeful

When Aly returned from the World Championships in Tokyo, the 2012 Olympics were only about a year away. She was beginning to believe that if she stayed healthy and continued working hard and performing well at competitions and in training camps, she would have a chance to compete at the Olympics.

That year Aly had to make some tough decisions. Since her eighth-grade year, college gymnastics coaches had been watching her train and compete, and they wanted Aly to make a decision about where she would one day attend college. Aly was excited about the coaches and gymnasts at the University of Florida, and she thought she would one day compete in gymnastics for

Aly once dreamed of attending the University of Florida in Gainesville.

the Florida Gators. But while she was at the World Championships in Tokyo, people began talking to Aly about becoming a professional gymnast. This would mean that Aly could earn money for participating in interviews, photo shoots, and events to promote gymnastics. But she wouldn't be allowed to compete in college gymnastics anymore.

Aly set up meetings with a few different agents—people who work with athletes to coordinate professional opportunities. In the end, Aly decided she would become a professional gymnast instead of attending the University of Florida. She was excited about the opportunities that would be available to her as a pro. One of her first professional engagements was a photo shoot for the clothing brand Ralph Lauren. Aly had always been interested in fashion, so the photo shoot was a dream come true.

Aly also made another decision about school that year. Many top athletes choose to complete their schooling online so they have more time each day to train. But Aly and her parents and coaches believed that it was important to attend school. Aly enjoyed being able to attend classes and be social with her friends like a normal teenage girl.

For years, Aly had been going to some high school classes in between training sessions at the gym and completing other classes online. When she went to competitions or training camps, she would ask her teachers to give her work to do while she was away. But for her final year of high school, Aly decided to take all of her classes online instead. This would free up more time for training. Aly was sad that she wouldn't be able to see her school friends very often anymore, but she and her friends understood that she needed to make some sacrifices to achieve her goals in gymnastics.

A Busy Season

For the next several months, Aly spent her time working out and practicing in the gym, attending photo shoots or other events to promote gymnastics, and working on homework when she wasn't doing something gymnastics related. The day after her eighteenth birthday, Aly competed at the US Classic and came in first in the all-around. That spring she was able to take a night off from training to attend her high school prom. The day of her high school graduation, Aly was off to the 2012 National Championships in Saint Louis, Missouri. Aly was third in the all-around. Jordyn Wieber came in first, and Gabby Douglas was second.

Finally, at the end of June 2012, it was time for the Olympic trials. At the end of this two-day competition,

From left: Kyla Ross, McKayla Maroney, Aly Raisman, Jordyn Wieber, and Gabby Douglas made up the 2012 US Women's Gymnastics Team.

Martha Karolyi and the Olympic selection committee would choose five women from the US national team to make up the US Olympic team. Aly was nervous. She badly wanted to make the Olympic team. She had worked hard and performed well in competitions over the last two years, but she knew nothing was guaranteed. Many other talented gymnasts were on the national team, and they all wanted a spot at the Olympics.

Aly came in third in the competition. When it was over, the national team went into one room, and the selection committee went into another. Several minutes later, the selection committee reached their decision and announced the 2012 Olympic gymnastics team. Gabby Douglas, McKayla Maroney, Kyla Ross, Jordyn Wieber, and Aly Raisman had made the team. Aly was going to the Olympics!

Fierce Five

July 2012 found Raisman and her teammates—who called themselves the Fierce Five—in London, England, on display before the world as the United States' top gymnasts. Shortly after the US team had been selected, its members had voted to name Raisman their team captain. So just as at the World Championships in Tokyo, Raisman would be the team leader.

The Olympic gymnastics competition included several events. First, everyone competed in a qualifying round. This round determined which gymnasts would later compete in the all-around final and in the event finals. There would also be a team final. The top twenty-four gymnasts in the qualifying round would go on to the all-around final, and the top eight on each event went on to the event final. But only the top two gymnasts from any country could compete in these finals. Even if all five US gymnasts finished in the top twenty-four,

Raisman smiles after a strong performance in the 2012 Olympics.

only two would be able to compete in the all-around final.

Many people in the media expected Douglas and Wieber to compete in the all-around for the United States. But Raisman did well in the qualifying round. She stayed focused and calm in every event. In the end, she finished in second place overall, behind Viktoria Komova of Russia. Douglas was third, and Wieber was fourth. Douglas and Raisman would move on to compete for the United States in the all-around final.

Gabby Douglas was a favorite of casual fans and gymnastics pros alike in 2012.

Raisman was excited to be in the all-around final, but the team final came first. She and her teammates wanted to win gold in this event. They knew they could stay focused and work together to reach their goal. On the day of the team final, the Fierce Five cheered as they each completed excellent routines. They encouraged one another when they became nervous. They reminded one another that they had all trained hard for this day, and they all had the skills and abilities they needed to do well.

Proud Parents

When Raisman competed in the Olympics, everyone in the United States learned her name and watched her on TV each night. They also watched Raisman's parents. NBC's broadcast of the qualifying round showed footage of them sitting in the stands, watching their daughter compete on bars. They were nervous and tense, and they swayed their bodies in time with her routine. When she finished, they looked completely relieved. The video went viral overnight. Audiences had loved seeing Raisman's parents reacting to her routine.

When they saw the video later, Raisman's dad was embarrassed, but her mom thought it was funny. They were both incredibly proud of their daughter. "We know how long and how hard she's worked, literally every day for the past fifteen years," Raisman's father

Raisman's parents, Lynn and Rick, have always been among her biggest supporters.

said. He also noted that, as nervous as they were, watching Raisman compete at the Olympics brought them "pure joy."

The last event in the team final was floor, and Raisman was the last to perform her routine. It was a crowd-pleasing routine filled with difficult skills, set to the Hebrew folk song "Hava Nagila." Raisman liked the song because the audience could clap along. It was also a nod to her Jewish heritage. She knew that if she performed well, her team could be Olympic champions.

As soon as Raisman finished her routine, her teammates began jumping up and down and cheering. They all believed her routine had been good enough to earn them the gold medal. But they needed to wait for the judges' scores to be sure. Raisman and her teammates held hands as they waited. As soon as the score appeared, the team cheered, and Raisman broke into tears. She was an Olympic gold medalist.

More Success

The Olympic all-around final was two days later. Raisman felt more pressure for her individual events than she had for the team final. Raisman finished vault and uneven bars strong. But before her beam routine, she became nervous. She almost fell off the beam. She knew it hadn't been her best performance, and Raisman thought she had lost her chance of winning an all-around medal.

At the end of her floor routine, Raisman looked at the scoreboard. She was tied for third place with Mustafina. To break the tie, the judges looked at their three best scores. Mustafina's were higher, and Raisman finished in fourth place. Raisman was disappointed to have missed out on a medal. She felt as though she had let herself and her country down.

Raisman's Olympics weren't over yet. She had made the event finals in both beam and floor. But

Aliya Mustafina is a star of Russian gymnastics.

Raisman was becoming tired from the strain of Olympic competition, and she was disappointed about her all-around finish. She worked hard to stay focused for her other events. Beam was first. She finished well, but when she looked at the scoreboard, she saw that she had come in fourth again.

However, Bela and Martha Karolyi were in the stands, and they thought her score was too low. Brestyan asked the judges to take another look at Raisman's routine and her score. A few minutes later, the judges raised Raisman's score—which put her in another tie for third place. This time, Raisman won the tiebreaker and the bronze medal.

Judaism and the Munich Eleven

After Raisman's gold medal routine on floor, an Israeli reporter asked the gymnast if she wanted to dedicate her performance to eleven Israeli athletes who had been murdered in a terrorist attack at the 1972 Olympic Games in Munich, Germany. The 2012 Games were the fortieth anniversary of this event. Raisman said yes. She also publicly expressed her support for an idea raised by the victims' relatives to have a moment of silence for them at the 2012 Games. The International Olympic Committee opted not to have the moment of silence, but Raisman's support meant a lot to those who'd been in favor of it.

Raisman was one of nine Jewish athletes on the US Olympic team in 2012, and she was proud to speak out on an issue that mattered to many in the Jewish community. She later said, "I realized after the 2012 Olympics that when I compete, I'm not only representing the USA but also representing the Jewish community, and that's something special to me."

Since then, Raisman has become the most famous Jewish athlete in the world. Her Jewish heritage is important to her. When she was growing up, she enjoyed attending events at her temple with her family, and she has always loved celebrating Hanukkah. "Being Jewish is all about spending time with your family," Raisman has noted. "I love when we get together for the holidays."

From left: Jordyn Wieber, Gabby Douglas, McKayla Maroney, Aly Raisman, and Kyla Ross celebrate on the podium after winning the gold medal.

Raisman's final Olympic event was floor. She was nervous. She wanted to make part of her routine easier so she wouldn't risk falling or making a mistake. But Brestyan told her that he knew she could do the difficult routine. She had trained hard for this day, and he knew she could succeed.

Raisman went for it. She completed her complicated opening tumbling pass and stuck the landing. From then on, she didn't feel anxious or nervous. She felt powerful. Raisman finished her Olympics with a second gold medal, and she became the first American woman to win gold on the floor. All of her hard work and determination had paid off.

Making a Comeback

Immediately after the 2012 Olympics, Raisman had some
time off from gymnastics for the first time since she was
very young. She could travel and go on vacation, and
she didn't have to spend hours in the gym every day. She
did have some publicity business to attend to once the
Games came to a close. She and the other members of
the Fierce Five went to New York for TV appearances and
photo shoots. They also went to the MTV Video Music
Awards, and they visited the White House. Gymnastics
were a part of the team's publicity tour as well—the
athletes performed gymnastics shows in forty cities across

Members of the 2012 Women's Gymnastics Team meet President Barack Obama at the White House.

the country. But because they weren't competing, the performances weren't nearly as intense as the Olympics had been.

Raisman did some of her own speaking events and photo shoots too. In addition, she designed a line of gymnastics leotards. And Raisman even got to compete on the TV show *Dancing with the Stars*. She came in fourth in the competition, and she loved having the opportunity to connect with people in a new way. She enjoyed being able to express her emotions through dance in a way that gymnasts don't do in their routines.

Future Plans

In the year following the Olympics, reporters began to ask Raisman about her plans for the future. They wanted to know if she was going to continue training in gymnastics and whether she would compete again. They especially wanted to know if she would try to compete in another Olympics. Raisman was enjoying her time off, and she knew she had already accomplished a lot in her gymnastics career. But sometimes she wondered what might have happened if she hadn't been so nervous in the all-around final.

In 2013 Raisman and her Fierce Five teammates were inducted into the USA Gymnastics Hall of Fame. After the event, Raisman and Brestyan talked about her career. Raisman's first international meet had been in Brazil, and they knew that the 2016 Olympics would also be held in Brazil. They thought it could be fun to finish her career in the same place where it began.

Brestyan warned Raisman that returning to gymnastics would require a lot of hard work. She would need to be even better than she had been at the 2012 Olympics. Raisman thought she could do it. She realized there was more she wanted to accomplish. In 2014 Raisman began spending long hours in the gym once again.

For three months, Raisman ran and did jumping and strength exercises. She needed to build up her strength and endurance before she could safely try any of her old skills. Raisman also knew how important it was to take care of her body. She began working with doctors and nutritionists to learn how to properly fuel her body. She learned that she had to eat lots of carbohydrates and protein. When she ate the right foods, her body felt better, and she had more energy during her training sessions.

When Raisman returned to training camps at Karolyi Ranch, she made sure to give her body time to rest and recover. She insisted on getting plenty of sleep, and she relaxed by drinking tea and giving herself facials. By this time, Raisman had some new teammates, including the bubbly Simone Biles. When Biles saw Raisman napping and drinking tea, she came up with a new nickname for Raisman: Grandma Aly.

A Tough Year

In 2015 Raisman returned to competition. She and Douglas, who had also returned after the 2012 Olympics, competed in Italy. Raisman finished third in the all-around and on floor. It felt good to be back.

The rest of 2015 was difficult for Raisman. She felt enormous pressure to do as well as she had in 2012. She was nervous before meets, and she had a hard time perfecting her skills in practice. At the 2015 World Championships in Glasgow, the US team won gold, but

Raisman failed to qualify for the finals in any individual events.

Adding to the stress, a private investigator came to interview Raisman. Some of the other gymnasts on the national team had brought complaints before USA Gymnastics about the national team doctor, Larry Nassar. They questioned his treatment methods and said he had been touching some of the gymnasts inappropriately. The private investigator wanted to know if Raisman had had similar experiences.

The questions surprised Raisman. Although, looking back, she recalled that Nassar's treatments had sometimes made her feel uncomfortable, she hadn't considered before now that she may have been abused. "I thought only strangers could hurt me," Raisman later explained. "I never imagined . . . what [Nassar] was doing was really wrong." Nassar often framed his inappropriate touching as a specialized form of treatment for back pain. In addition, Nassar would often buy coffee and other treats for the athletes under his

Gymnast McKayla Maroney experienced frequent abuse while being treated by Larry Nassar.

care. He offered sympathy when gymnasts complained about their coaches. He tried to make athletes believe he was their friend. So Raisman wasn't sure what to say in response to the investigator's questions. But as she thought about it some more, she realized that Nassar had touched her inappropriately too. She realized she'd been a victim of abuse. The realization was devastating.

USA Gymnastics told Raisman not to say anything about the Nassar investigation. The situation made her even more anxious. She was concerned that the media might find out about it and start asking her questions. She wasn't ready to talk about it publicly yet.

In December 2015, Raisman faced a different kind of challenge. While practicing her floor routine at a training camp, she landed a skill and felt a pop in her left foot. It immediately started swelling. She returned home to see her doctor, who said she had partially torn the ligaments in her ankle. He recommended that she take four weeks off to heal. If she didn't stay off her ankle, she risked injuring it more, which would require surgery. If she needed surgery, there wouldn't be enough time to recover before the Olympics.

Even though she had to stay off her ankle, Raisman worked out in the gym every day. She did exercises to strengthen her arms and core. More importantly, she worked on getting her mental focus back. Raisman's family knew she needed help remembering how good she really was. They showed her videos of her routines in London and reminded her that she needed to believe in

Raisman has trained hard at Brestyan's over the years.

herself. By the time her ankle healed, Raisman had gained some of her confidence back, and she was able to take some of the pressure off herself to be perfect all the time. When she returned to competition in 2016, she was able to give her best effort, and her results were much better than they had been in 2015.

In July 2016, Raisman competed at the Olympic trials. She reminded herself that she didn't need to be perfect. She remembered her mother's advice that it's more important to be a good person than to win gold medals. This helped Raisman stay calm. In the end, she was chosen to be on the Olympic team along with Douglas, Biles, Laurie Hernandez, and Madison Kocian. Once again, Raisman's dedication had paid off.

Redemption

In Brazil, Raisman's teammates selected her to be team captain. This year, just as in London, the media didn't think Raisman would qualify for the all-around. Instead, they expected Biles and Douglas to compete. But in the qualifying round, Biles finished first, Raisman second, and Douglas third. Biles and Raisman would be advancing.

First, they competed in the team final. The team had won the qualifying round by almost ten points, so they felt confident. They knew that if they performed the way they knew they could, they would come away with the gold medal. Biles was the last to perform. When she finished her high-flying floor routine, the team waited for her score to appear and make their victory official. Then they huddled up and announced the team name they had chosen

Raisman's elegant floor exercise routines have won her acclaim.

Martha Karolyi gives Raisman a celebratory hug.

in honor of Martha Karolyi's final year as national team coordinator: "We are the Final Five!"

Two days later, Raisman put on a bright red leotard with matching lipstick. She and Biles were ready, and Raisman believed she could do well. Raisman began on vault and then moved on to bars. She did well on both. But just as she had in London, she began to get nervous before her beam routine. She worried that the same thing that had happened in London would happen again. This time, Raisman managed to stay focused and calm, and she completed a clean routine. Floor was all that was left, and she knew she was in position to win a medal. The years of hard work, frustration, and training of her body and mind came together to help her win the Olympic silver medal in the all-around.

From left: Aly Raisman, Madison Kocian, Laurie Hernandez, Gabby Douglas, and Simone Biles wear huge grins after winning gold.

Then she had one last Olympic event: the floor final. As in the all-around, Biles won gold, and Raisman came away with another silver. She had now won six Olympic medals, the second most of any American gymnast. She was proud of her accomplishment. "It's not something that people expect or that's easy to do after taking a year off and having it be a second Olympics or being the grandma, as they like to say," Raisman said. "I'm happy I proved everyone wrong."

More Important Than Medals

As she had four years earlier, Raisman set off on a whirlwind tour with her Olympic teammates. They made appearances on TV shows, did photo shoots, and had interviews. This time, Raisman focused on sharing her message of strength and body positivity. She said that when she was younger, some of the kids in her class had bullied her for having big muscles. She used to be ashamed of her muscles, and she would try to cover them up. But eventually she realized that without her muscles, she couldn't do gymnastics. She realized how important it is to be confident and proud of her body.

Raisman speaks during the Glamour Celebrates 2017 Women of the Year Live Summit.

Raisman participated in photo shoots that showed off her strength, and she talked about how much she appreciated her body. "I thought I was in the best shape of my life in 2012," she said, "but it was even better now." Raisman planned to continue training and try to make the 2020 Olympic team too.

But in November 2017, Raisman released her book *Fierce: How Competing for Myself Changed Everything.* In the book, Raisman tells the story of how she became a successful Olympian. She also publicly revealed that Nassar had abused her. Raisman spoke about this abuse in interviews with *Time* magazine and *60 Minutes.*

By January 2018, about 300 other people had come forward, saying they had been abused by Nassar. In court, before Nassar was sentenced to up to 175 years in prison, Raisman and more than 150 others shared statements about their experiences. At the beginning of her statement, Raisman said, "We are here. We have our voices, and we are not going anywhere." She spoke for about twelve minutes. She said she was disappointed in Nassar for abusing his position as a doctor and for manipulating

Raisman makes her victim impact statement about Larry Nassar.

so many young girls. Raisman also called out the US Olympic Committee and USA Gymnastics for not acting more quickly to address the accusations and put an end to the abuse. She said she hoped USA Gymnastics would investigate the situation and

Raisman and other survivors of Nassar's abuse were honored with an Arthur Ashe Courage Award at the 2018 ESPY Awards.

make sure that abuse like this never happened again.

Raisman would go on to file a lawsuit against USA Gymnastics and the US Olympic Committee. She also partnered with the organization Darkness to Light, which advocates for the prevention of child sexual abuse. Raisman challenged parents, coaches, and other adults involved in youth sports to complete training to learn how to protect kids.

Training for the 2020 Olympics is no longer Raisman's top goal. Instead, she is focusing on the issue of sexual assault in gymnastics. "I love the Olympics and being able to represent my country," she said. "But with everything going on right now, I realize that this is more important than any gold medal."

IMPORTANT DATES

1994   Alexandra Rose Raisman is born on May 25 in Needham, Massachusetts.

2004   She begins training at Brestyan's American Gymnastics Club.

2009   She competes at her first international competition, the Junior Pan American Championships in Brazil.

2010   She competes at the World Championships in the Netherlands.

2011   She competes at the World Championships in Tokyo, Japan.

She decides to become a professional gymnast.

2012   She makes the 2012 Olympic team and competes in the Olympic Games in London, England.

She becomes the first US woman to win Olympic gold in the floor exercise.

2013   She competes on *Dancing with the Stars*.

She and her London teammates are inducted into the USA Gymnastics Hall of Fame.

2014   Raisman begins training for the 2016 Olympics.

2016   She is selected for the 2016 Olympic team and travels to Rio de Janeiro, Brazil, for the Games.

2017   She releases her book, *Fierce: How Competing for Myself Changed Everything*.

She reveals publicly that she was abused by national team doctor Larry Nassar.

2018   She reads her victim impact statement at Nassar's sentencing hearing.

She partners with Darkness to Light and dedicates herself to advocating for victims of sexual abuse.

SOURCE NOTES

9 Justin Hathaway, "Aly Raisman Cries Tears of Joy the Second She Wins Olympic All-Around Medal," *NESN*, August 12, 2016, https://nesn.com/2016/08/aly-raisman-cries-tears-of-joy-the -second-she-wins-olympic-all-around-medal/.

22 "Aly Raisman's Parents, Ricky and Lynn Raisman, Respond to Being Viral Video Stars," Huffpost, July 31, 2012, https://www.huffingtonpost.com/2012/07/31/aly-raisman -parents-rick-lynn_n_1723529.html.

22 "Aly Raisman's Parents"

25 Curt Schleier, "Question & Answer: Aly Raisman," *Hadassah Magazine*, January/February 2018, 64.

25 Curt Schleier, "Aly Raisman on Abuse: 'Society Is in Desperate Need of Change,'" *Hadassah Magazine*, November 2017, http://www.hadassahmagazine.org/2017/11/15/aly-raisman -sexual-abuse-society-desperate-need-change/.

31 Elizabeth Narins, "Aly Raisman Speaks Out about Larry Nassar's Sentencing," *Cosmopolitan*, January 19, 2018, https://www .cosmopolitan.com/health-fitness/a15391587/aly-raisman-larry -nassar-sexual-abuse-doctor/.

35 "Why the USA Women's Gymnastics Team Named Itself the 'Final Five,'" *Fox Sports*, August 9, 2016, https://www.foxsports .com/olympics/story/why-is-usa-womens-gymnastics-called -the-final-five-gold-medal-080916.

36 Chris Chavez, "Olympic Silver Medal a Symbol of Successful Comeback, Redemption for Aly Raisman," *Sports Illustrated*, August 11, 2016, https://www.si.com/olympics/2016/08/11 /aly-raisman-rio-olympics-gymnastics-all-around-silver-medal.

38 "Aly Raisman 'Keeps Getting Better with Age,'" NYBlueprint, September 8, 2016, https://nyblueprint.com/sports/aly-raisman -keeps-getting-better-age.

38 Mahita Gajanan, "'It's Your Turn to Listen to Me.' Read Aly Raisman's Testimony at Larry Nassar's Sentencing," *Time*, January 19, 2018, http://time.com/5110455/aly-raisman-larry-nassar-testimony-trial/.

39 Steve Helling, "Will Aly Raisman Compete in the 2020 Olympics? 'Speaking Out Is More Important Than a Gold Medal,'" *People*, February 7, 2018, https://people.com/sports/aly-raisman-2020-olympics-larry-nassar/.

SELECTED BIBLIOGRAPHY

Brady-Myerov, Monica. "Gymnast's Journey: Toddler Tumbler to Golden Girl." *NPR*, May 16, 2012. https://www.npr.org/2012/05/16/152752207/gymnasts-journey-toddler-tumbler-to-golden-girl.

Chappell, Bill. "Aly Raisman Becomes First U.S. Woman to Win Olympic Gold in Floor Exercise." *NPR*, August 7, 2012. https://www.npr.org/sections/thetorch/2012/08/07/158364638/aly-raisman-becomes-first-u-s-woman-to-win-olympic-gold-in-floor-exercise.

Chavez, Chris. "Olympic Silver Medal a Symbol of Successful Comeback, Redemption for Aly Raisman." *Sports Illustrated*, August 11, 2016. https://www.si.com/olympics/2016/08/11/aly-raisman-rio-olympics-gymnastics-all-around-silver-medal.

Fouriezos, Nick. "Aly Raisman Is the #MeToo Hero That American Sports Needed." Ozy.com, January 26, 2018. https://www.ozy.com/need-to-know/aly-raisman-is-the-metoo-hero-that-american-sports-needed/83485.

Grigoriadis, Vanessa. "'This Is Bigger Than Myself': How the Women of the U.S. Gymnastics Team Found Their Voice." *Vanity Fair*, Summer 2018. https://www.vanityfair.com/news/2018/05/how-the-women-of-the-us-gymnastics-team-found-their-voice.

Hutchins, Andy. "How Aly Raisman Lost the Women's All-Around Bronze Medal on a Tie-Breaker." SBNation, August 2, 2012. https://www.sbnation.com/london-olympics-2012/2012/8/2/3215545/aly-raisman-bronze-medal-tiebreaker-womens-all-around-gymnastics.

Jenkins, Sally. "Aly Raisman: Conditions at Karolyi Ranch Made Athletes Vulnerable to Nassar." *Washington Post*, March 14, 2018. https://www.washingtonpost.com/sports/olympics/aly-raisman -conditions-at-karolyi-ranch-made-athletes-vulnerable-to -nassar/2018/03/14/6d2dae56-26eb-11e8-874b-d517e912f125 _story.html?noredirect=on&utm_term=.cd7fb043702c.

Park, Alice. "Aly Raisman Opens Up about Sexual Abuse by USA Gymnastics Doctor Larry Nassar." *Time*, November 13, 2017. http://time.com/5020885/aly-raisman-sexual-abuse-usa-gymnastics -doctor-larry-nassar/.

Park, Andrea. "Aly Raisman Might Skip the 2020 Olympics to Fight Sexual Abuse." *TeenVogue*, February 7, 2018. https://www.teenvogue .com/story/aly-raisman-2020-fighting-sexua-abuse.

Raisman, Aly. *Fierce: How Competing for Myself Changed Everything.* New York: Little, Brown, 2017.

FURTHER READING

BOOKS

Goldman, David J. *Jewish Sports Stars: Athletic Heroes Past and Present*. Minneapolis: Kar-Ben, 2014. Read this book to learn more about Aly Raisman as well as other Jewish athletes who have made history.

Ignotofsky, Rachel. *Women in Sports: 50 Fearless Athletes Who Played to Win*. New York: Ten Speed, 2017. Check out this book to read the stories of fifty women athletes, including gymnasts Nadia Comaneci and Simone Biles.

Lawrence, Blythe. *Great Moments in Olympic Gymnastics*. Minneapolis: Sportszone, 2015. Learn more about incredible Olympic moments and athletes such as the Magnificent Seven and Gabby Douglas.

Luke, Andrew. *Gymnastics*. Broomall, PA: Mason Crest, 2017. Read about the history of gymnastics, from its origins as a military training exercise to one of the world's most popular sports. Use QR codes inside the book to watch videos of some of the sport's most iconic athletes and routines.

WEBSITES

Alexandra Raisman on Twitter
https://twitter.com/Aly_Raisman?ref_src=twsrc%5Egoogle%7Ctwcamp%5Eserp%7Ctwgr%5Eauthor
Get a glimpse into Raisman's life through the words and photos she shares on Twitter.

Aly Raisman
https://usagym.org/pages/athletes/athleteListDetail.html?id=97680
Find information about Raisman's career and watch videos of her gymnastics routines.

Darkness to Light

https://www.d2l.org/

Learn more about the organization Raisman is working with to put an end to abuse.

USA Gymnastics

https://usagym.org/

Read news and information about USA Gymnastics and the current national team members.

INDEX